INTRODUCTION

Novels take a long time to write, right? They are lengthy, highly detailed stories, crafted with intricate layers and complicated levels. Many an author has slaved for years, even decades, to get their novel written. And here I am telling you that you can write a novel in 30 days? Even if you've never written anything before?

Yes.

And what's more, here I am telling you that writing a novel, or attempting to write a novel in thirty days, is one of the most powerful and liberating creative pursuits a writer can ever dream of.

WHAT IS A NOVEL?

I define a novel as a lengthy piece of narrative fiction with a minimum of 50,000 words.

Most mainstream commercial novels fall at around 60,000-70,000 words. If that target definition feels more comfortable for you to define a novel, then have at it and call this a novella writing challenge.

50,000, in my writing experience, is a magical number for a book. It's long enough to detail an intricate story, but not too long to fluff it out with extra, often needless padding, to meet an arbitrary definition. After all, the standard length of books was only defined by the best spine width to be noticed on a bookstore shelf. We live in a different world now.

50,000 words is also an achievable number to fit into a month long challenge.

1667 words a day. It's workable for most of us, even in the midst of a busy, stressful life. 1667 words also isn't terribly hard for most of us to catch up on, ~~if~~ *when* life gets in the way of writing.

WHY WRITE A NOVEL IN 30 DAYS?

High intensity, faced paced writing is not for everyone. Yet, I implore every writer, or would-be writer, to try a novel in a month challenge at least once.

Why?

Because writing a lot in a short period can do incredible things to your creative brain.

Writing so much in such a small block eliminates the luxury of perfectionism. The inner critic doesn't have time to see what you're up to on the page, let alone try to stop you making a mistake. When you're writing at a fast and furious speed, it's just you and your creativity, your raw words, and the beautiful essence of your most authentic story.

By choosing to write a novel in thirty days, you're embracing a whirlwind of creativity, passion, fun, and literary mayhem. You're given permission to write less than perfect prose, to play and see what happens, to get out of your own way and write your book.

A novel in a month challenge is not just about writing words. It's an exercise in optimistic, ambitious persistence that, for many of us, ends up being a transformative journey that rejuvenates the writing spirit, forges a solid writing practice, and delivers a sense of accomplishment like nothing else.

But yes, writing a novel in thirty days is also quite difficult.

WRITE YOUR NOVEL IN A MONTH

THE NO-STRESS GUIDE TO DRAFTING A NOVEL IN THIRTY DAYS

KATE KRAKE

THE CHALLENGES OF THE THIRTY DAY NOVEL

From the creative (writer's block, unruly characters, and unfathomable plot holes), to the physical (aching hands and wrists, stiff backs, necks, and shoulders, eye strain, brain drain); the emotional ("I'll never be good enough to get this done!" "This writing is so terrible!"); and the social ("When will I ever see my friends again?" "Why can't my family give me ten minutes of quiet writing time?")—the struggles and pitfalls of participating in a 50K in 30 days writing challenge are plentiful and vast.

But don't despair!

Each struggle is worth the value that this endeavor brings, and this survival guide will help you navigate the downsides, optimize the upsides, and cross the finish line with minimum pain and stress, and maximum joy and creativity.

True, some authors take years to write novels, even the first draft. If you're this type of writer and a thirty-day novel seems like the last thing you'd want to think about, then go, freely create and write in the way that feels best to you.

But, if you're tired of second guessing your creativity, if you're desperate to unleash the shackles of perfectionism and let raw creative momentum take over your words and see what happens, and you want to get your book finally finished, then I'll show you exactly how to get it done.

MY HISTORY OF 50K IN 30 DAY WRITING CHALLENGES

I have written over twenty novels using the method outlined in this book. Nine of those novels are currently published and more are in the process of revising for publication.

Like many fast drafting authors, I started this process as part of the NaNoWriMo events.

If you choose to take this challenge during the official NaNoWriMo (National Novel Writing Month) events, then go for it. But you don't have to have any affiliation with NaNoWriMo to write a 50K novel in a month, nor do you need to complete the challenge in November. You can choose any thirty day block that suits you to conquer this lofty literary goal, and you can choose to go at it on your own.

I've written a variety of genres in different word-processing apps. I've also written my 50,000 by hand. I've written while moving interstate, twice. I've written with no kids. I've written while pregnant and terribly ill. I've written with babies on my lap, and toddlers sleeping, or typing next to me on toy computers. I've written while injured. I've written while dealing with chronic dizziness and vertigo. I've written with joyful enthusiasm and I've written with mournful despair.

I've stopped at exactly 50,000 words on day 30. I've hit 50K words on day 10. I've written as high as 85,000 words (by handwriting!) in 30 days. I've set goals under 50,000 and still called it a win. I've written as a strict "this counts as a novel" rule follower, and I've penned 50,000 word collections of short stories and even nonfiction following these same principles. I've also started many timed writing challenges like this and not completed them.

Hitting the 50K finish line or not, when it comes to smashing out lots of words in little time, I've seen and done it all.

And now I offer that experience to you so that you too can experience the thrills of high-velocity novel writing, and hopefully avoid the pitfalls.

A Note About Brains

As already mentioned, this form of challenge is not for every writer. For some, it is the only way they can write. Long after I embraced my first novel in a month challenge, I learned I have a different type of brain to the majority of the population. It's clear to me now that the strengths afforded to me by my neurodivergence make novel in a month writing sprints more suitable to me. I think very quickly (not always coherently!), so story structures tend to flow out of my fingers quite freely. I get bored with ideas very quickly too, so for me, mulling around on projects for a long time usually results in unfinished projects. That's likely another reason the 50K target length appeals to me over longer novels. I hyperfocus, meaning I can give deep attention to one task with unwavering focus and hit extreme productivity under the right conditions. There are, of course, a lot of downsides to this kind of thinking, especially when it comes to fitting in a novel writing month around all the daily comings and goings of living in the world and having kids. I also burn out quickly, so I have to be careful about my energy and health.

I am not saying that only neurodivergent folk are suited to high productivity creative writing challenges. I am also not saying that all neurodivergent folk are suited to it either.

It's all about learning what works best for your creativity and your cognition style, no matter what your neurotype is.

This book covers everything you need to know to get you from the enthusiasm of day one and that first sentence, through the drudgery of the middle weeks, when thirty days seems like forever and your novel is a steaming pile of word goop, all the way to the glorious finish line and beyond.

So, loosen up those muscles, pick up your pen or fire up your writing software, and let's dive into the exhilaration that only a manic creative challenge can bring.

You owe the world your novel. You owe yourself your novel. The universe needs you to do this.

Let's go.

CHAPTER 1
THE NOVEL IN A MONTH MINDSET

Before you even start thinking about genre or plots or characters or writing tools or how you're going to find time in your already busy life to write 1,667 words every day for a month, it pays to work on your mindset.

Your author mindset is the most important resource you have to get your word count high enough to reach the finish line on time and see you through the month with a minimum of stress.

Success is all in your head.

Go into the month thinking how difficult or impossible it's going to be, it's likely to prove difficult or impossible.

Go in thinking how fun and wild and wonderful it's going to be, it's likely going to be fun and wild and wonderful.

Yes, this is a tough challenge.

Yes, it's going to take a massive chunk of your time and energy every day.

Yes, your family may revolt. You might even revolt yourself. Get ready for it all, and commit to keeping on writing.

This intense writing endeavor is the best kind of hard work. It's hard work that feeds your soul, hard work that gives you a reward of infinite value at the end.

Are you ready to earn that reward?

THE FIVE KEYS OF THE SUCCESSFUL NOVEL IN A MONTH MINDSET

A high word count + low time writing challenge will always be about quantity-over-quality literary abandon.

We fast drafting authors strive for imperfection; we ignore our inner critics and let whimsical creativity run wild. We have fun. Start the month with this mindset and you're already on your way to winning.

Remember these five Novel in A Month mindset keys:

1. It's a Rough Draft, Not a Novel
2. Write Fast, Don't Look Back
3. Follow the Fun
4. Abandon the Shoulds
5. It Doesn't Matter

1. It's A Rough Draft, Not A Novel

On day 30, you won't have written a novel.

That's not to say that you will not write 50,000 words of fiction. You will.

You're going to write a fun and messy first draft. I call this the Alpha Draft. Or to use Anne Lamott's phrase, it's "a shitty first draft."

Your Alpha Draft has every chance to become a novel later, with editing and polishing.

You will not write a novel during your 30 days; you will write the foundations of a novel. The very strong, very reliable, very honest foundations. And that's where every novel starts.

The novels you've read look nothing like the rough drafts they were born from. Novels are developed with careful revision. Drafts can be, and in my opinion are best written with the opposite.

Think of this Alpha Draft as the first scribblings of basic shapes an artist uses to start their picture. In the beginning, those circles, lines, and weirdly positioned rectangles don't look like much of anything, but as the artist works to add shade, form, and perspective, they transform those rough shapes into a masterpiece.

That's how we create novels, too. With foundations of rough words (that may or may not make much sense). It's only in the revision stages that a real novel emerges and the masterpiece arrives.

Your fast drafting month is not for revision, so let those rough forms scatter across the page and live for what they are. Beautiful, solid, literary foundations.

2. Write Fast, Don't Look Back

This writing challenge is a masterclass in fast drafting.

Fast drafting is when you write the whole first draft of your novel, start to finish, as fast as you can. Write first, think later.

Fast drafting is incredibly liberating.

Fast drafting means no editing, not even for typos. What? You can't even fix a typo? Nope, not in my fast drafting rules. Others say it's fine to fix typos—I say, "Why bother?" That's next month's problem.

You can write in fully detailed scenes. You can write in scenes that just contain the dialogue or other basic details. It's up to you.

If you encounter something you need to research, make a note, keep writing, and do the research later.

I even do this for yet-to-be-decided character names, using placeholders like <<FMC>> (Female Main Character) and <<BADGUY>> throughout my Alpha Drafts. The <<>> is so I can find them easily when it's time to fix it all.

The Two Writing Brains

Writing a novel requires two different and opposing parts of your brain: the creative, free, experimental, daring, playful part; and the editing analytical, serious part. Fast Drafting is all about that first part.

This entire process means you need to let go of your inhibitions and ideas of right and wrong and "good" writing. You need to permit yourself to be a crappy writer because, in the beginning, we all are crappy writers.

You need to get into a flow state where you don't even notice your fingers moving across the keyboard as your literary world feels like a reality.

Every time you edit, you take your brain out of this creative flow mode and pull it back into the rigid world of rules and analysis. This is your editing brain, and it has no place in your 30 days. Stories don't get created with your editing brain. They get revised and refined.

Unfortunately, this is the same part of the brain that will tell you that everything you do is rubbish, that this whole idea is a waste of time, and you should just quit now and get back to your real and important daily life. Do you want that brain in charge during your special 30 days?

No.

So, switch off your editing brain.

How?

Write fast.

Keep writing, as quickly as you can before your analytic mind and inner critic get a chance to catch up.

Write and write and hold nothing back.

If the editor brain does pop in as you're writing (and it will), tell it politely, "I'll listen to you next month. For now, Creative Freedom Brain has the floor, so please, get out of the way. You'll have your turn to shine, I promise." And then carry on making a spectacular mess.

---

3. Follow the Fun

From word 1 to word 50,000, and even before if you're pre-planning your novel, let this be your mantra:

"Follow the fun."

To get the most out of it on every level, your 50K in 30 days event should be an abundantly positive and optimistic experience. For the entire month, your focus needs to be only on the delight of storytelling.

Writing stories is fun! So don't forget to experience that fun at every turn.

If your story gets stuck, how can you make it more fun? This may or may not involve doing dastardly things to your characters. Or putting in some weird and whimsical, spontaneous element just for fun.

How can you make the writing process itself more fun?

Try teaming up with writing buddies, online and offline. Set micro goals and reward yourself with something fun. Wear a weird and wonderful outfit while you write to get into the zone. Invent a special writing happy dance. Whatever rocks your world.

Writing a novel isn't a terrible chore. It's not drudgery to take a chunk of time out of your life and dedicate it to literary fun and creativity. It's a privilege and a choice. So enjoy it.

Follow the fun and you'll not only feel good and smash your word count goal, but you'll also produce a story filled with passionate enthusiasm. And that makes for good writing.

We get more into fun in the What to Expect chapter coming up.

4. Abandon the Shoulds

Writing fiction is a deeply personal experience. And while many authors write novels in 30 days, it is always a different thing for each of us.

Many a writer takes up their words on day 1 to establish a writing habit, or revive a lapsed writing habit. Some are completely new writers, never written a word, and take a blind leap into the world of writing to see what they're capable of. Some 30 day novelists are old pros and use the momentum of the formal challenge to get ahead on their next novels, or to test the waters on new ideas. Others just become writers for a month, because there's something creative bubbling away inside and they want to see what it's like to let it out for a while. I'm sure there are thousands of other reasons to take on such a demanding challenge.

What's your reason?

Whatever it is, it's right. And you're setting the right goals and working toward them in the right way.

So ignore all those *shoulds* out there telling you to do it one way or the other. And, yes, that includes this book if something I advise here doesn't sit well with you.

You *should* write 50,000 words.

Negotiable.

You *should* start a new project on day 1.

Not necessary.

You *should* get to the end of the story on day 30.

Helpful, but negotiable.

You *should* not edit as you write.

Again, helpful, but some do edit as they go and still do fine. So, negotiable.

You *should* have fun doing your writing month however you like and reward yourself suitably when you reach your goal.

Okay, this one you definitely *should* do.

5. It Doesn't Matter

Your novel matters a whole lot in various ways. Your writing process matters too.

Yet, when the struggles invariably hit during the month, remember that none of it matters.

Not really.

Your novel and your creativity and your writing life are incredibly valuable, sure. But that value is not linked to your personal value.

It's a rewarding challenge, yes. But that reward must not come at the cost of your physical or mental health.

If you have to stop, or slow, or change your approach or whatever else you need to do, then so be it. It doesn't matter.

There's no failure anywhere in this challenge.

If you can only manage a thousand words or ten words, that's still a win. The whole point of the challenge is to push yourself and make words that didn't exist last month. "Winning" is relative.

Nothing bad is going to happen if you don't reach 50K. I've started multiple drafts that never made it to the finish line. Oh well. The world didn't end. No one got hurt. It doesn't matter.

CHAPTER 2
HOW TO PREPARE FOR THE CHALLENGE

There are two general philosophies on how to get ready for the day 1 starting line.

1. Prepare in advance.
2. Show up on day 1 and start thinking about your story for the first time.

I've done both, and I generally do better with the Prepare in Advance approach.

That said, there are benefits and downsides to both approaches.

Benefits of No Advance Novel Prep

Coming into a large, thirty day writing challenge with no previous preparation is an exercise in intense creative liberation. You just don't know what's going to happen in either your story or your writing practice. You throw caution to the wind and just see what comes out.

A fast drafting practice will create a lot of mistakes. The work gets rough. So, with no preconceived ideas of what a story idea will look like when fleshed out to a novel size, this write first think later approach can be quite effective at silencing the inner critic even further.

There's also a lot more room for play and discovery with this method. You just follow your words and ideas as they happen down whatever curious rabbit hole that arises on the page. That said, these rabbit holes can lead to some dark, scary places...

Drawbacks of No Advance Novel Prep

Deep, dark plot holes, creative burnout, writer's block, ideas that seemed like a good idea at the time but won't form into a cohesive narrative.... Even those who plan ahead encounter these, and many more difficult moments.

When you're writing to a tight deadline, getting stuck takes away from your writing time. If you don't have any pre-prepared ideas to follow or fall back on, it's easy to lose time trying to find a way out.

When we get stuck in any of the many writer's pitfalls, it's common to suffer a confidence lag. If you're flailing around in the bottom of a "how do I make this idea work?!" pit of despair, watching your thirty days tick by and your word count stagnate, it's easy to lose hope that this wacky challenge is even possible let alone worthwhile.

If you don't advance prepare your story, at least advance prep your life by clearing the decks as much as possible.

WHY PREPARE LIFE IN ADVANCE?

Some amount of forethought is a powerful tool to have in your kit.

Preparing for the month ahead isn't only about setting out the ideas for your story in advance. It's about planning your entire life so that your intense writing challenge will be supported from every angle.

The month will bring struggles, and there'll come times when having a clear schedule, the support of a team, and knowing what to write next will be a blessing.

You don't need to spend a long time preparing. You don't need a full-blown outline of all of your story beats. Thinking about what you're going to create, making a few notes, and organizing your non-writing life can be enough.

THE TEN KEYS TO PREPARE FOR WRITING A NOVEL IN A MONTH

(in no order of importance)

1. Know that it's possible
2. Choose a month
3. Clear the decks
4. Embrace imperfection
5. Consider a writing buddy
6. Ready your tools
7. Decide on your story
8. Plan something special at the starting line
9. Plan something special for mini-goals along the way
10. Plan something special for the finish line

1. Know That It's Possible

You might be worried that your life is too busy to add such a nutty pursuit as writing a novel in a month into it. Why set yourself up for failure? Many have this fear.

Every writer's life is different. Some have no kids and seemingly endless time to write. Some *are* kids and have seemingly endless time to write. Some have kids, many kids. Some have day jobs, and busy careers, and caring responsibilities, and chronic illness, and high support needs, and so many other elements that are there, making 1,667 words a day seem impossible.

One of my writing friends has a million kids (actually, just nine. Nine!) and works a full-time, demanding day job. They write at night and have penned multiple novels. I don't say that just because this writer does it one way, that's the way you should do it too. But just know that it is possible. Against all odds, against all demands, regular folk with incredibly busy lives *do* write novels in a month.

If you want it, make it work. It will take some management, experimentation, negotiation, but you can work it out. At least give it a go. See what happens. You might surprise yourself.

2. Choose A Month

It's up to you when you position your 30 days.

It can be a calendar month, or you can choose any thirty-day block of time that works for you.

You might like to consider the seasons when you decide when you'll be writing. Do you go out less in winter, and therefore able to get more writing time at home? Or does your energy lag in winter, and you'll be better off waiting for a vibrant summer?

Whatever time you choose, try as much as reality dictates to ensure there's not too much else happening that month. Which brings us to…

3. Clear the Decks

Some people say the busier your life, the better your chance of reaching 50K.

In my experience, no. Not even close.

I like to clear out the month as much as possible. Have everything settled as much as reality allows, have life routines in place. Know in advance (as much as possible) what's happening in the month. Plan how you anticipate working around these distractions.

I've tried this in the middle of moving house. Not recommended.

I've tried this at the beginning of the school year when I *thought* life would be easier since the kids were back at school. But I forgot about the increase in mental load at a twice daily school run, and the endless demands life brings while everyone is getting into the routine. Settle the routines first. Find some headspace.

Tell your family what you're doing and why it's important and why they have to fend for themselves for thirty days. If you'd prefer to write in secret, find your secret writing time in advance and perhaps get your cover story in order.

Still, things *always* come up. This goes a millionfold if you have children! Illness, random events, mechanical failures, work stuff, kid stuff, pet stuff, all the life stuff. Roll with it as best you can.

4. Embrace Imperfection

Intentionally and joyfully lower your standards. This goes for your creativity and all other areas of your life.

Try loosening control, even just temporarily. Relax your grip on what "good" novels look like, on what "good" writing reads like. Let housework slide as much as it's sanitary to do so. Put nonessential work demands on the back burner. Prime yourself for imperfection in whatever way you can and get ready for the mother lode of imperfection that you're about to create on day 1 of your challenge.

5. Consider A Writing Buddy

What's better than pursuing an arduous yet zany fun literary challenge?

Doing it with a friend.

If you're a part of a writing community, or have writerly friends, consider taking up the challenge together.

You might even consider getting a non-writer to join you on this. A contained challenge like this is an excellent project for anyone who has always wondered about writing but hasn't yet found the momentum or motivation. Who knows? An invitation from you to join your writing whimsy might change someone's life and turn them into a lifelong writer.

Going at it as part of a team provides the solidarity you'll come to lean on when times get tough.

It's an unfortunate reality of the world that there are actually few people around who will see the joys and pleasures of writing like this. Taking the challenge with a kindred spirit will also give you someone to celebrate with, someone who truly gets what this is all about when you cross the finish line.

Also, a little bit of friendly, race to 50K competition can go a long way to boosting your motivation.

6. Ready Your Tools

Before day 1, check your writing gear is in order.

Embarking on a creative writing challenge like this is an excellent excuse to buy yourself some fresh notebooks. Does a writer ever need an excuse to buy new notebooks?

Typing? Ensure your word machine is ready and reliable. Know your backup methods. If you're planning to work with a new program, especially if it's Scrivener, get to know how it works ahead of time.

I have written three novels by hand (so far). So if you're handwriting your opus, get a stack of your favorite writing books ready. If you're a "favorite pen" kind of writer, have a pile of them prepared in advance. I'm a fountain pen geek, so an ink stockpile is always required. There's more about handwriting novels in Chapter Three, Writing Tools.

7. Decide on Your Story

We've already covered the pros and cons of prepping a story in advance, but I do feel that even a modicum of advance prep is a key to success.

You don't need to have a meticulous plot outline ready to go at the beginning of the event. Some do, and that's great.

At the least, it helps to know your genre, know the primary characters, and know the basic plot. Titles can wait. "Untitled [Insert Your Genre] Novel" is a perfectly acceptable working title.

To get further ahead, know your character arc. This is the internal and sometimes external change your characters go through. If you've got an idea for a character arc, the plot essentially takes care of itself.

You might also want to learn a bit of basic narrative theory.

No, you don't need to have memorized the entire Hero's Journey or *Save The Cat* structure, but understanding the basic form of a story will go a long way in keeping you on track during the month.

If you're keen, write up a formal outline before day 1.

Warning: Don't go overboard on writing craft theory. Learning too much might plant too many *shoulds* in your mind that could threaten the entire philosophy of embracing imperfection during the event.

8. Plan Something Special at the Starting Line

Find what treasures work for you to fuel your enthusiasm. New pens and notebooks are a great way to start the month with something special (again, do we ever need an excuse?!). For some, it could also be sweet treats or giant vats of coffee, or simply a morning alone to start your manuscript.

Whatever you like to do, mark the momentous event of day 1 to reinforce the fact that you're taking the first steps on a truly special journey.

9. Plan Something Special for Mini-Goals along the Way

Plan how you'll reward yourself as you go along. Ready treats for completing word count sprints, treats for big round word count numbers, treats for the halfway point, treats for getting through a bad day, and of course...

10. Plan Something Special for the Finish Line

A mammoth effort deserves a mammoth reward. Whatever floats your boat, be sure to float it.

Sure, having written 50,000 words in thirty days is a reward in itself, but the external prize makes it all the sweeter.

A pre-planned prize for the end can also work as a dangling carrot, tempting you ever closer to the finish line. What do you love? Give it to yourself with joy and pleasure. You deserve it.

Should You Start A New Story?

What's best?

Starting a new story from scratch on day 1?

Or

Continuing an existing story and letting the 30 day momentum push it to the end?

Either. You can write whatever you like.

BUT...

Beware.

Some writers, especially those new to the fast drafting process, have a great deal of trouble with the whole "write first, think later" mentality when working on an existing piece.

A work in progress might already be laden with expectations and a certain quality that could get in the way in the pursuit of creative mess making during the month.

It can be a more rewarding, less pressured creative practice to start fresh with a new idea on day one. As with all things in writing, it's all up to you, but be aware of this potential mindset pitfall.

CHAPTER 3
WRITING TOOLS

What you use to bring your novel to the page is as unique to you as the story you're writing.

You might already have your favorite novel-writing tools. During the challenge, it's a good idea to stick with what you know so you don't have to waste writing time learning new tech.

If you want to make a change before your designated day 1, or you're a totally new writer with no writing kit experience, here are a few suggestions on good word-making tools. As mentioned, get to know any new software before day 1.

WORD PROCESSORS

Scrivener

Scrivener is a word-processing software designed especially for writers. It easily organizes long-form writing projects using folders and documents, providing space to keep notes alongside your drafts. With Scrivener, all of your chapters and scenes, however you choose to divide your work, are displayed alongside your drafting screen so you can jump around easily, change the order of things, and always see where you're up to. There's also a corkboard feature if index cards are your thing, and you can even color-code sections in a variety of ways.

Scrivener also has a Project Target function that comes in super handy for a word count and time-based challenge. You set your overall word count goal (50K), set your deadline (30 days), and it tells you how many words you need to write that day. This is extra helpful for when/if you fall behind and need to recalculate your daily 1,667.

Scrivener comes with a variety of templates, including one for novels, but I prefer working with the blank template and have developed my custom system over years of use.

Many complain Scrivener is too hard to use and takes too long to learn all the functions. Yes, there are heaps of features, but Scrivener is only as complicated as you need it to be. I've been using Scrivener for almost fifteen years and still only skim the surface of all of its capabilities. There's no need to learn everything before you start—simply choose a template, familiarize yourself with the layout and how to add a new document, and start writing, picking up what you need to know when/if you need to know it.

At the time of writing, Scrivener is available for Mac, iOS, and Windows. No Android yet.

Why Can't You Use MS Word or Google Docs, Pages, Etc.?

You absolutely can, and many do. But…

The problem with these traditional word processors is that they have a linear view and only one document per file. You need to scroll through hundreds of pages when you want to backtrack into your book. Some work around this by using formatted headings in the navigation pane, but this is still not as useful as what Scrivener allows.

yWriter

If you're unable to or not sure you want to invest in Scrivener, yWriter is a similar program (though far more basic). At the time of this writing, it's free.

yWriter was developed by Australian author, Simon Haynes, and you know a program designed by an author is always going to best serve an author's needs.

NOTE-TAKING TOOLS

How will you capture those story ideas before and during your month?

Even if you don't record every idea as it comes along, having a note-taking system on hand is valuable.

Digital or analog or a combination of the two?

You will have your own preferences, and one is not better than the other, although digital might be more convenient for most, for obvious reasons.

Most phones have native note apps, and there are millions of others you can install. I like Microsoft's OneNote. Others prefer Evernote. Google Keep is a simple alternative.

Some brains work better with analog tools. A small notebook in the handbag or pocket works just fine. Others use index cards. Many an idea has been captured on a napkin or receipt. When you're writing fast and thinking faster, any way you can capture your ideas will do.

HANDWRITING

I have fast drafted multiple novels by hand. One of them was 85K words, and while that story is still yet to reach the revision stage (and may never!), it's still my most wordy manuscript ever.

If you're considering handwriting your novel, get some practice before day 1. Your hand contains thirty-four muscles and a bunch of other things, and all of those things will hurt a lot if they don't get some solid training before they embark on this thirty-day marathon. So, start writing a lot by hand.

Learn some hand stretches to do along the way because even if you prime your paws, hand cramps will still happen.

I recommend using a free-flowing ink. I'm a fountain pen devotee and did all my hand novels with different fountain pens. Fountain pens are also valuable as they don't require the same downward pressure of a ballpoint, so can sit nice and loose in the hand, reducing cramping. They're also really pretty! If you don't use fountain pens, gel pens are good too.

Paper choice will depend on what kind of pen you use. For fountain pens, the paper should be smooth enough to let the pen glide easily, but not so slick that the ink smudges. You don't have time to wait for ink to dry! Avoid rough, thirsty paper too, as not only will it absorb way more ink (and have you refilling more often) but the ink may also leak through the pages. Some rougher papers can also build up gunk in your pen nibs.

Your paper doesn't need to be fancy. My favorite writing books are ordinary, spiral-bound notebooks (A4 size here in Australia) which, depending on the brand, typically cost less than five dollars each. I find there's less pressure to fill pages with quality writing when using a cheaper notebook.

Take some time to experiment with the best paper-and-pen combo before day 1, and have a stack of your pens, inks, and papers of choice ready to go.

Handwriting ergonomics are just as important as keyboard positions.

I handwrite with my page propped up at an angle on a firm clipboard. This reduces wrist pain and hand stress and lets my arm move more freely. Your body might have other requirements. Experiment with various positions before the starting line.

Whatever your writing position, be sure to move around regularly. More on this in Chapter Seven.

CHAPTER 4
WHAT TO EXPECT

Even though fast drafting a novel in a month is a unique experience for every writer, there are a few elements that most of us can expect to encounter during the challenge.

Very Loud Self-Doubt

Even though we're all there to write very messy Alpha Drafts and tell those inner editors to shut up for a month, self-doubt is real, and it happens to most of us.

It could be a doubt in your writing abilities. It could be a doubt that you'll make it to the finish line. Whatever breed of self-doubt creeps into your writing experience, don't let its presence put you off.

You *CAN* experience self-doubt and *STILL* write your way through to remarkable achievements with a mindset of fun and frivolity.

Acknowledge that little negative voice. What's it telling you? Hear it. Respect it as a voice of fear that's only trying to protect you. Thank it. Now tell it to shush. You've got writing to do.

Fun!

We've already touched on the fun mindset, but here's more of what to expect from the fun of the challenge.

What's so fun about pushing your mind and body to extremes to reach a massive word count goal in a small time? Well, nothing... if you don't know where to look.

The fun of this challenge comes in the fact that it's a BIG goal and, yes, it's a bit crazy to put your life on hold to reach for it (even crazier *not* to put your life on hold and do it anyway).

The fun comes from letting your plot run away with the fairies (and if you want those to be actual fairies appearing in your story, then have fun with that too!).

It's fun to watch a story evolve out of nothing.

It's fun to watch prose (albeit messy prose) fill in the gaps in the outline you've been working on before the start.

It's fun to throw away that outline and explore the hidden depths and unimaginable heights of your creativity.

It's fun to play word sprints with fellow writers, or even yourself.

It's fun to set yourself up with a series of chocolatey rewards (or your treat of choice) and then write your way to sugary goodness.

Pain

Back to the not-so-great. Here we're talking about physical pain. A lot of authors suffer from writing related aches. Hands hurt, wrists hurt, arms, neck, shoulders, backs, eyes hurt. One month, I developed an excruciating pain in my elbow, thanks to the way I sank into my desk chair as I wrote. It only took a couple of days to injure, but even after I changed my system, the damage was done and took another month to heal. My writing life as a whole has given me a wrist tendon situation that I have to keep on top of with keyboard alignment, a vertical mouse, wrist supports, and different arm exercises. That wrist always flares when I delve into fast drafting challenges if I don't protect it from the start.

Storytelling might happen in our heads, but it's our bodies that actually need to get the words out into the world.

So treat that body with respect.

Stretch it. Move it. Massage it. Exercise it. Feed it right. Rest it.

Support it or medicate it where necessary. Move it more. Your word count will thank you for it. There's more on this topic in Chapter Seven.

More Ideas than You Know What to Do With

Ideas and creativity are curious and amazing phenomena—the more you use, the more you have. As you write, even if you're following an outline, more ideas will come to flood the page. Not all of them will be suitable, but you can always save them for another project.

No Ideas at All

While there are some days when your ideas will just appear out of your fingertips by some marvelous magic, there are other days when, like a not-so-marvelous curse, your story just doesn't want to show up, and every idea sucks, and you've forgotten how even to word. Sorry, but you still need to write on those days.

Don't worry. If/when you go back to read and edit your novel after the month, it's a surprising thing that the words you wrote on your worst days tend to look exactly like the words you wrote on your best days.

Comparisonitis

It's completely natural to compare yourself to what other writers are doing or have done, especially in a challenge like this.

Some people can write more than 1,667 words a day. Some cannot reach that and tailor this month long challenge to a more manageable number. Some write with a dozen kids hanging off their keyboards. Others write in complete solitude every day. Some wing it from the first word. Others write something they've been planning forever. You'll compare yourself to everyone else. It's just what humans do. We don't have to listen to that comparison, though, and especially we don't have to suffer from it.

Share experiences and learn with and from other writers. But there's absolutely nothing to be gained by comparing yourself to other writers and feeling that you're lacking in the difference.

Especially don't compare your Alpha Draft writing to any kind of published writing. Not published books, not "works in progress" posted on blogs or social media. These published works are not Alpha Drafts. Even the bits and pieces posted online as "rough drafts" are still almost always polished to some degree, and will look a billion times better than the muddy Alpha Draft words you're smashing out on any given day during your challenge.

You're writing what you need to write, how you need to write it. If you must compare, compare yourself to yourself the day before, and even then, remember that good and bad days happen in equal measure.

Everything Else Can Wait

It will surprise you just how much of your regular life you can let go of during your monthly challenge. You may temporarily function on less sleep, you can definitely watch less TV, read less, talk to your family less, use your phone less, and how about a monthlong social media hiatus?

A challenge like this is an excellent lesson in resetting expectations of life, in shaking up systems, seeing how much mess you can tolerate, and letting your partner learn how to cook for once. Remember, imperfection.

Ebb and Flow of Energy between Weeks

When we condense the novel drafting process into a month, we experience it as a microcosm of the typical energy flow writers go through to get a novel done. While for most writers, that happens over months or years, we're condensing it into days and weeks. Enthusiastic starting energy, sagging drudgery, exhaustion, and then relieved and elated finishing energy is the general pattern. We'll get into more of these ebbs and flows over the four weeks in the next section.

This isn't an exhaustive list. As I keep saying, every writer is different, and every novel is a different. Even if you've done novel in a month challenges before, every month will be different. Whatever the four weeks throw at you, you'll get through it with attitude, perseverance, and words. Lots and lots of words (and don't forget to stretch and move!).

WHAT TO EXPECT: WEEK ONE

Starting Energy

Week one of the challenge typically starts on a high.

You're excited. You're overflowing with enthusiasm and optimism and perhaps a sugar or caffeine rush.

On day 1 (at midnight if you roll that way), the figurative starting gun fires, and you're off.

I'll never forget the first time I took a 50K in a month challenge seriously, my second attempt at such an event. After a "failed" first attempt, I was hooked on the idea of achieving the goal and desperate to make it to 50K to prove I could. I had written little at that stage of my life, definitely not a novel, but I was determined this was about to change.

It was approaching midnight, the day before my chosen start. I was so excited and knew my story was going to be brilliant. I typed the first few words and my stomach fell into a pit as those young words revealed what a terrible writer I really was. I fiddled around with those opening lines trying to get it right, get rid of that pit feeling, and it took me days to get into the flow of fast drafting quantity before quality and for that disappointment to disappear.

I reached 50K in that month, but only because, after those first agonizing days, I let go of expectations and followed the fun. That story started life as a high-brow literary coming-of-age piece and morphed into a horror-comedy romp set in a pub overrun with zombies. Total fun. Did I publish it? A resounding <u>NO</u>. Will I ever read it again? Unlikely. Still, I have never learned more about my creative writing process than I did that month, and I have that first terrible novel to thank for every novel I have written and published since.

Just go with those first words, no matter how good or bad they are.

Chances are they're not as good or as bad as you think anyway, but that's a next month problem. Let your story grow with whatever your brain throws out. Let yourself grow as a writer alongside it.

For now, just ride that wave and remember:

FUN!

If you're writing with buddies, in week one, you'll see others' word counts creeping up. Resist comparisons!

It's sometimes fun to race other writers, using someone else's count as a target to beat. BUT, I would only recommend this if A: that person is not a standard 5K+ a day writer (they exist!) B: you're comfortable enough in the Fast Drafting mindset not to let this race mentality defeat you and fall into a mess of feeling like you're a failure if you don't win.

Week One Top Tip

Build a buffer.

Try as much as you can to use that raging starting energy to exceed your daily baseline 1,667 words. Building a nice cushy word count buffer in week one will help a lot for what's around the corner.

WHAT TO EXPECT: WEEK TWO

Losing Momentum

The shine will probably wear off this week.

We're not fully into the drudgery phase yet, but by the end of this week, you might feel your energy wane.

Creative writing is incredibly taxing, especially if it isn't something you regularly do. Your brain gets exhausted like any other body part and it's been working at 110 percent capacity for a week. Fatigue might also set in if you're getting less sleep to meet your word count goals.

There are some rare and special souls who will hit their 50K this week (or even earlier). If you're one of them, well done! Now bandage up your hands. If you're not, don't fret. This is not the usual. You're doing well.

Keep hitting that baseline, and more if possible. If you've built yourself a padded word buffer in week one, try to save it for the end of this week going into week three.

Week Two Top Tip

Resist Shiny Object Syndrome.

Around this time, your plot might get out of control, or lost, or you hate it so much it feels like an insult to the entire history of human storytelling.

Surely it's not worth continuing? It's not too late to start a new story, is it?

Many writers get hit with Shiny Object Syndrome in week two. It's the siren's call of the new story, the new idea, something better.

You've started making a word mess (a.k.a. writing a novel) and it's getting really ugly in there. The temptation to burn it to the ground and start fresh with something new is a real thing. I've certainly felt it and succumbed to it.

DON'T DO IT.

At least not in this challenge. Outside the month, it's a different situation. Here, just keep writing.

That new story seems so shiny and devoid of problems because you haven't started making it into words on the page yet. It's just an idea. The messy story you're ready to break up with also started life as a shiny new idea, resplendent in all its perfection. Now look at it! It's all wordy and jumbled and lost and... ARRGH!!!

The same thing will happen to the shiny new idea you're tempted to run away with. It happens to every idea.

Let the story evolve into whatever it evolves into, and you can only do this by seeing it through to the other side of the mess.

New and emerging writers are often quite good at writing beginnings. But since many a new writer gives up when the continuingly complicating plot gets the better of them, they might not have a lot of experience writing middles and ends and all the narrative complexity that brings. Week two brings you that experience.

Just keep going.

Remember: FUN!

WHAT TO EXPECT: WEEK THREE

Urgh

This is the hardest week. At the start of it, at least.

You're tired. You've hit the halfway point, but there's still a long way to go.

Have you used up your word buffer yet? If not, take a rest and let yourself slide to the daily baseline, or below if you're tracking ahead.

It's usually best during this stage to at least write a little every day, even just fifty words, rather than opt for the whole day off. Momentum is a Fast Drafting writer's best friend. But if you're really struggling, a whole day off might be best, even if it means you fall behind.

Keep on keeping on.

Employ some of the word boosting tactics in the next chapter. Word sprints are brilliant for this low-energy time.

Lean into your community. Find support from writing buddies who are feeling or have felt the same.

Around this time, your real-life family and friends, and maybe your boss, might get sick of this whole writing malarkey. "Are you *still* working on that thing?!"

Just ignore them. Be patient, be kind. Keep ignoring them. Keep writing.

No one but another writer can see the epic journey that you're on, and the metamorphosis of spirit that is continuing with every word.

It might feel really bad right now, but remember, before a caterpillar turns into a butterfly, inside that cocoon they break down into a mushy mixed-up goop. Think of your messy Alpha Draft as that goop, and keep writing until you get your beautiful wings.

You're nearly there! The wheel is about to turn, and with it, your energy.

Week Three Top Tip

Be extra kind to your body, mind, and soul. Take a walk. Just a ten-minute stroll will typically serve all three.

WHAT TO EXPECT: WEEK FOUR

FANFARE!!

You're Almost There!

It's time to muster and bring this baby home.

Welcome to finishing energy.

Finishing energy is the last sprint toward the finish line. You can see it. You're so close. Pull out everything you've got and hold nothing in reserve.

You've got this.

If you're writing a 50K word story, you're writing to the end of the plot. If your novel is shaping up longer than our target, keep going with wherever you're at.

Many a writer will reach their win before the end of this week. If this isn't you, remember, you are under no obligation to finish before day thirty.

Week Four Top Tip

Have that finish line reward ready. Visualize it as you blast (or limp) through those final words.

When you're done, exhale, smile, hug yourself, and get into that juicy prize.

You're a real-life novelist now.

Now sleep.

CHAPTER 5
WHAT TO DO IF YOU FALL BEHIND

Don't panic.

It happens to most of us.

If it's only a day or two of word count deficits, you can catch this up by writing more in the coming days until you're back on track.

If it's more, and you've missed entire weeks, you can go hard and catch up to the goal, if that's not going to harm or even kill you.

Recalculate how much you need to write each day in order to get to the finish line on time and spread the catch up over the rest of the month.

Alternatively, you could shrug it off and keep writing as best you can. Plenty of writers in these challenges declare their own word count targets below 50K and still claim it as a win.

Have fun.

It doesn't matter.

CHAPTER 6
TACTICS FOR BOOSTING WORD COUNT

In my many years of doing novel in a month challenges, I've seen just about every word count padding trick in the book. I've met writers who write stuttering or deaf characters so they can repeat a bunch of words. I've seen writers with characters who fill in the plot for other characters, via copy and paste. I've heard of characters who liked to quote long passages from other books (watch out, copyright!).

There's a fine line in a zany pursuit like this between writing an imperfect and messy draft, and writing nonsense or superfluous crap. It's up to you what you want to count as "writing," and, yes, some writers do count copy and pasting duplicated prose.

If that's how you're going to roll, and still call it a win, that's fine. Just be prepared to do a lot more editing and writing if you plan to sit down to turn your 30 day effort into something real after the month.

Before you resort to any potentially dodgy tactics to hit the word goal, ask yourself:

Are you here to type 50,000 words, or are you here to write a novel draft?

AI Writing Tools

Forget thirty days. With AI text-generating tools, you can engineer novel draft in thirty minutes. Even less.

It's up to you if you use AI to contribute to your word count.

I am generally pro AI tools as amazing advances that help authors reach new heights with their careers.

But would I use ChatGPT for this challenge?

To help me generate ideas? Maybe.

To actually write my book? No.

Remember, there's a big difference between an AI-assisted author and a person who engineers books with generative AI and has the bot write the text.

Engineer or author. Which do you want to be?

Without resorting to the interesting tactics listed above, or getting an AI to churn out your words, here are other, far more legit ways to boost your word output.

Write at the Right Time

What's your most energetic time? For many, it's first thing in the morning. Others, late at night. Follow your individual chronotype and hit your big words during your cognitive sweet spot.

Use High Quality Tools

Use fast tools. Ditch the old clunky keyboards and laptops that take forever to load. Use software that lets you work through your manuscript intuitively. If you're handwriting, avoid ballpoint pens. Read the Writing Tools chapter for more ideas.

Do Word Sprints

Sprint.

Set a timer. Ten to twenty minutes is ideal. Five works. Thirty might be too long.

GO!

Write as much as you can as fast as you can. When the timer goes, stop. Rest. Marvel at your max wordage. Repeat.

Word sprints are powerful medicine, so only repeat a few times a day. Most of us can't sustain that kind of insane output for long, and we don't want to burn out the engines before the finish line.

Word sprinting is extra fun if you're running with your fellow writers, maybe as a race or maybe just for camaraderie.

Write What You're Excited About

There's no reason to write a novel in linear order. Try writing the exciting scenes first, the ones you know are going to be great and can't wait to get into. For most of us, these are the scenes that come fastest with the most ease. How about an entire novel made up of super exciting scenes?

Write on the Go

Instead of being tied to your desk during writing times, become a mobile writer.

Gather portable tools like a laptop, tablet, phone, or notebook, and embrace the flexibility to write whenever you've got a few minutes. Whether it's done in a café, a park bench, or a library, waiting in line, waiting to pick up your kids, commuting on the train, whenever, this flexible approach to writing time can add hundreds, even thousands of words you might never have gotten down if you were waiting for dedicated desk time.

Use Dictation

Dictation means speaking your words and letting the computer turn them into type. It can be super fast.

Most new computers and tablets have voice-to-text functions now, as do some phones. There are free (e.g., Speechnotes) and costly (e.g.,

Dragon) apps to capture your words, and they all work with varying ability to the same effect.

Dictation isn't for everyone. It takes a different part of your brain to send your ideas out of your mouth instead of your hands. Since most of us learned to capture storytelling with our fingers, this can be a tricky transition and takes some getting used to. If you're interested in trying dictation, try it out before day 1.

Also, depending on your dictation software, be aware that a dictated scene might take an extra-long time to edit. I can now laugh about the time I spoke thousands upon thousands of words into a Dictaphone and had Dragon translate them to text. Every time I commanded "new line" (to format a new line of text), Dragon typed "urine." Hilarious, but one of many pains to edit.

Don't Delete a Single Word

If you're writing along and something just isn't right, don't delete it. Put that text in italics or change the font color to mark it for later deletion. For thirty days, every single word written counts toward your goal, even the ones you already know won't make the final novel.

Do Wild and Unexpected Things

Either in real life or to your characters. Both is also good.

Make giant reckless decisions for your characters, and send them into impossible situations. Write yourself into a corner so that the only way out is a fighting explosion of creativity. It doesn't matter how outrageous and implausible, just go with what feels fun and powerful and wordy.

Visualize your readers when the novel is done reading this mad scene and thinking, "Wow! I did not see that coming! Awesome!"

CHAPTER 7
LOOKING AFTER YOUR BODY

For the four weeks of your challenge, you'll likely be so busy concentrating on your stories and your rising word count that there's every chance you'll forget, neglect and even harm your most important writing tool—your body.

I've seen it done and even done it to myself.

As writers, we are so often living in our heads that we forget that head is part of a body—a body that needs to be taken care of properly in order for it to function well. And this function includes writing.

This challenge is extreme sport for writers, and just like any athlete, we need to take care of our bodies. If not, pain happens, illness happens, exhaustion happens. And then words don't happen.

Writing-related injury and other health issues are common. Here are some ways to keep your body happy and healthy while still getting that word count through the roof.

Move

Sitting for long periods does nasty things to our bodies. A standing desk is often touted as the cure for desk workers (that's us), but standing up for long periods can pose just as many health risks. It's the lack of movement, locking into one position, that's the real problem, not sitting, not standing.

Move around while you write. Sit, stand, sit on the floor, lie on the floor, cross-legged, outstretched, kneeling, standing on one leg, standing on the other leg, rocking back and forth, squatting, lunging. Get creative with it and keep changing position.

Stretch

While you're moving, throw in a few stretches. Pay particular attention to the areas between the tips of your toes and the top of your head. See what I did there?

One of my favorite writing break moves, that's also an exceptional full-body stretch, is to do a few rounds of the sun salutation yoga sequence. It only takes a few minutes. Try it. Or devise a movement routine that suits whatever your body needs. Your word count and your body will thank you for it.

Sleep

Life can get turned upside down during a long haul writing challenge, and writers often find the time to write by sacrificing sleep. If this is you, proceed with caution.

Sleep holds the universe together.

Good sleep means a more productive, more focused writer. In writerly terms, that means a more focused, less frazzled author.

A bit less sleep can be okay in the short term, but even after just a few days, the negative effects will show up.

Rest

This includes sleep, but it's also important to take waking rest. These are the times when you step away from the word count, from the forums, from screens and word-making tools in general, from all kinds of work, and be a normal, unplugged human for a while.

This is the chance to let not only our bodies have a break from being word count machines, but also our fried brains.

Rest can look different. Sure, there's the couch-and-Netflix kind of rest, but there's also active rest like playing a sport, playing a board game, walking, gardening, any kind of hobby you enjoy.

Give yourself a serious rest and your ideas (and words) will bound back in your next writing session, propelling you to the finish line.

Eat

While you're wandering through your fictional worlds, don't forget to eat in the real world. This doesn't mean slamming Doritos and chocolate into your face as you type. Food is the fuel that makes our words, so optimize what you eat in order to maximize your wordy output.

I am a reformed chocoholic and have been known to use the sacred brown stuff as a dangling carrot reward for reaching my writing goals. Overall, though, my diet is fairly optimized. Less-than-healthy treats are fine. It's all about moderation.

Hydrate

Drink. No, not coffee (my other sacred brown stuff). Not soda or energy drinks. Not wine. Water. Drink water. Electrolyte solutions, if suitable for you, are quite good too (no, not Gatorade, but real electrolyte supplements). Herbal teas are excellent too, just watch the caffeine content.

A well-hydrated body is less prone to injury. A well-hydrated brain is better able to focus and perform. A well-hydrated writer is better able to write.

Hand and Arm Health (as Part of the Entire System)

We've already talked about the importance of moving, stretching, and resting, but particular emphasis needs to be made for hands and the other writing appendages. I've encountered dozens of writers (and I've been one) whose wordy efforts have seriously injured their hands, even for the long term. We're talking tendonitis, carpal tunnel syndrome, nerve entrapment, muscle strain, and lots more. Remember, it doesn't stop at hands. Hands are connected to wrists, arms, shoulders, neck. Even your feet and hands have a relationship. Look after the whole system.

If It Hurts, Stop

Don't ignore any aches, twinges, tingles, numbness, or pains of any kind in any part. They're signals that something in your body is on the way to getting hurt, if it's not already hurt. If you're getting any of these warning signs, it's time to move, stretch, and rest. No one wants their one month of effort to lead to years of debilitating pain. Seek professional opinions if the pains or niggles persist.

Socialize

Writers often go off the grid during big projects like this, holed away in dark corners, talking only to and for people who don't actually exist. This can be a lot of fun! But like everything else, it's all about balance.

Long periods of solitude can be a prime opportunity for loneliness, depression, anxiety and other mental health issues to creep in.

Remember to get out, connect, and stay grounded in the real world. This doesn't need to be in person if you don't feel like it or can't for whatever reason.

This might sound more in the realm of mental health than the more physical things in this chapter, but our mental and physical health are part of the same whole.

CHAPTER 8
MANAGING TIME AND STRESS

Writing a novel in a month may be a thrilling adventure, but it's also a demanding challenge.

The best way to manage its challenges is to organize your time and manage your stress. Why are these two factors brought together in one chapter?

Because so much stress in a timed writing challenge (and other areas of life) comes from feeling like you don't have enough time.

Thirty days is *PLENTY* of time to write 50,000 words. But only with careful time management.

Even then, stress will still hit. You don't have to suffer from it, though. Remember the adage "pain is inevitable, suffering is optional" and use these ideas to help stop stress from getting the better of you.

Find and Prioritize Your Writing Time

Before day 1, decide when you're going to do most of your writing. In the morning, before everyone else in your family gets up? At night, when they're asleep? Lunch breaks? Whenever works for you.

Stake your claim on that time slot and prioritize writing during that period. Don't look at email or social media before you start. Don't clean anything, don't check anything, don't do anything else in that time allotment, just write. All the other stuff can wait until 1,667 is done for the day.

Legit interruptions can and will occur. Attend as necessary if something is literally on fire or a loved one is bleeding.

Structure Writing Breaks

Breaks are essential for our brains not to wither into stressed-out lumps of misery before day 30.

Most writers work well with a twenty-to-forty-minute writing session, followed by a five-ish-minute break. Repeat for a few rounds and then take a longer break of up to sixty minutes. These quick sessions work wonders for both time and stress management. If this schedule doesn't work for you, set up your writing day in whatever writing-time-plus-rest-time chunks you have.

Most humans max out after about four hours of dedicated, intense cognitive work (a.k.a. "deep work") over the course of a day. That's four hours total, broken up with rests.

Ensure that your breaks are also benefiting your writing. That means moving your body, eating, drinking, relaxing.

Focus on Small Goals

While the overall goal is 50K, regularly remind your brain that total number doesn't happen in a day.

1,667 words a day is totally doable for most of us.

If that can't be done in one session, try two sessions of 834 words. Or four 417-word sessions.

If days come up where even the 1,667 is a stretch, adjust the goal. You might make it up later in the month, you might not.

Remember: it doesn't matter.

Celebrate Small Wins

Don't wait until the end of the month to celebrate your accomplishment with one big victory party. Set small targets throughout the month and celebrate every one of them. It could be a daily word count goal, it could be just showing up to the page and opening the manuscript with or without writing a single word.

Acknowledge your every effort and recognize yourself for the champion you are for even signing up for this adventure.

Plan and Outline

This does not apply to all writers, but for many, preplanning and outlining before day 1 is both a time-saver and a stress-saver.

With preplanning your plot, there's no time spent wondering what your characters should do next, no freaking out because you can't think of something to write.

Outlining is not for everyone, but for the newbies who haven't yet discovered how they work best, even a basic outline can provide the right support and even a boost.

Minimize Distractions

Weed out distractions as best you can.

Turn off notifications on your devices. Turn off your young kids... okay, maybe not, but at least make sure they're settled, fed, distracted, or even better, asleep or entirely absent before you start your writing session. Older kids and other family members can and will deal with you putting them in second place while you're writing.

Put your phone in a different room. Just the sight of our phones, even if they're totally silent with screens off, can trigger a ping of distraction and the insidious urge to CHECK SOMETHING! ANYTHING! Hide it far away.

Do Something You Enjoy

Every day, do something that lights you up. Something besides writing (that's a tricky one when you love to write!)

This aspect of self-care will look different for everyone. It might be a run, or reading a comic, cuddling your dog, or yoga, or boxing, or dancing the cha-cha while listening to death metal. It can be big, like climbing a mountain, or small, like watching a funny video.

Seek Support

You're never alone in the writing journey. Connect with fellow writers to share your challenges and successes. Offer support to others; you might be surprised by how much wise guidance you can share with another author.

Lean on your offline support networks, if you have them. These might be family and friends, or paid professional support like childcare providers, or therapists and counselors.

Be Flexible

Life happens, and the unexpected will disrupt your writing plans.

Be flexible and forgiving with yourself (and perhaps also those doing the disrupting!). If you miss a day or fall behind on your word count, don't dwell on it. Keep moving forward, always upward from wherever you are. Remember, it's never perfection, always joyful imperfection, and it doesn't matter.

CHAPTER 9
MAINTAINING MOTIVATION

Quitting

There may (or will?) come times during the month where you just don't want to write. Or you just don't want to complete the month.

It's always fine not to finish a writing challenge, but before you throw it all in completely, consider why you're quitting.

Perhaps you just need a break. Are you tired? Is your self-doubt getting too loud?

Take a rest and come back to the decision whether to totally quit when you're feeling more rejuvenated.

If you'd still rather do anything but finish, then go with a glad heart and a triumphant spirit, knowing that you wrote even a few words.

Sometimes knowing when we're at our limit and need to abandon ship, and then doing it is an act of self-care and bravery.

Other times, feeling like we're being pushed too hard and continuing anyway, recognizing that the urge to quit is just fear talking, is the type of self-care we need to grow.

Which one are you facing?

If you decide to carry on despite all the difficulties and continue writing to the finish line, read on for ways to keep motivated and stop this urge to jump ship from coming back.

Clarify Your Reasons

Why did you begin this adventure? What inspired you to want to write a novel this way? Connecting with your original motivation can reignite your enthusiasm and remind you why your story is worth telling.

Set Milestone Rewards

Set a word count milestone. 5K, 10K, 25K… whatever feels good to you. Use snacks, stickers, downtime with your favorite show, anything you like as rewards for hitting these markers.

These small rewards are constant positive reinforcement and give you something to look forward to as you're dragging those words onto the page.

Visualize Your Success

Imagine your manuscript as a real-life novel. Some writers go so far as to mock up book covers for their stories. Others create vision boards with all kinds of images symbolizing their ideal success. This tangible reminder of the end goal can inspire you to keep writing, especially when the going gets tough.

Write With Others

Taking part in group writing sessions either in person or online can create a sense of community and friendly competition, boosting your motivation. The energy of fellow writers is often contagious, rekindling your energy and getting motivation back on track.

Shift Your Writing Environment

If you're suffering from demotivation, consider changing up your writing space for a fresh perspective and feel. Move to a new room, write outdoors, perhaps use coworking spaces or libraries.

Share Your Progress

Sharing your progress with others can work as a motivational boost as your friends, family, and fellow writers cheer you on. Who doesn't like praise and encouragement?

Sharing your progress can also work as accountability motivation. When other people know what you're doing and what your goal is, you might be more likely to hit that goal to prove to them that you can. This kind of external accountability doesn't work for every writer, but try it and see what happens.

Connect With Writing Buddies

Use your writing buddies as your cheer squad. And cheer them along too.

Use Writing Prompts

Writing prompts, especially those unrelated to your work in progress, can be a great way to inject some motivating creative novelty into your work. A fresh idea, a fresh perspective, or just some extra element of fun could be just the thing you need to get over through any slow patches, but especially those around the middle of the month when both your plot and your energy are sagging. Check out www.writingpromptworld.com.

Reflect on Your Progress

Check in often with how far you've come. Look at your manuscript and marvel at all those words that didn't exist last month, and look forward to the novel that will exist after day 30.

CHAPTER 10
BOOSTING CREATIVITY

Creativity is one of my favorite words, one of my favorite concepts.

I love it because creativity is both a feeling and a practice. It's inspiration and motivation. It's the wonder of manifesting something that didn't exist before, the alchemy of pulling intangible thoughts through your fingers, into the word processor or pen, and one day seeing them turn into a real-life book.

Creativity is magic.

And it's also, sometimes, really, really, really hard to find and cultivate.

There will be times during your month when your creativity, as both a feeling and a practice, will be in the driver's seat. These are the good days. Ideas flow, stories evolve, distractions melt away, you feel like a miraculous spirit connected with the wonder of the universe, and the word count keeps on rising.

On the not-so-good days, creativity has given up and left the building. Or at least that's what it feels like. You feel anything but miraculous, and rather a lot like an old balloon, wrinkled and flat, and no fun at all.

That's when our basic drive and persistence have to take control of the wheel. Drive and persistence force you into your writer's seat to drag those reluctant words out. We feel terrible and our frazzled brains reach for any distraction no matter how tiny and banal (in fact, the more banal, the better—that's why social media exists), to take us away from the torture that is writing.

Both kinds of days are normal for any writer's life, and that goes tenfold for writers taking part in high demand writing challenges.

Even though the bad days are probably inevitable, there are ways to minimize their impact and possibly even lessen the chance of them turning up in the first place. Try these ideas to keep your creative spirit feeling fresh and eager.

Embrace Random Writing Prompts from Everywhere

When turning to writing prompts, you aren't limited to the usual written prompts. Everything and anything is a writing prompt.

What's on your desk? Out the window? Put it in your story. A stranger on the bus this morning could be a new character. Something your kids say is your core theme. A Wikipedia article. An advertisement. The way the light shines on a leaf. Absolutely anything you see, feel, touch, taste, smell, hear, and think is a creative prompt.

Change Up Your Writing Routine

Shake up the creative flow by doing something different with your writing routine. Write at a different time of day, a different place, use a different tool. Sometimes, this change can be enough to unlock new ideas. Other times it might prove such a distraction that you're so relieved when you get back to the usual routine, your creativity switches on again.

Brainstorming

If you're out of ideas, or just need to inject some novelty into existing ones, try a brainstorming session. Even if you're in the middle of a plot and fairly sure you know where it's going, generating a bunch of new possibilities can put your creative mind into overdrive. You could find new connections from what you've already written, or conjure up a different trajectory that's so much better than the original. It might also turn out that you find your initial ideas are still the best and can keep on rolling with them, feeling confident and motivated.

Embrace Arbitrary Constraints

Writing 50K words in thirty days is a constraint in itself, but what if you tried setting arbitrary limits on what you can and can't write in a session?

Write for twenty minutes using only a character's senses to describe the scene. Limit those senses to one or two.

Write a chapter with only dialogue and no attribution tags.

Constraints can inspire novel thinking (no pun intended) and lead us to unique solutions to existing problems, or simply shake up our thinking patterns.

Change the Point of View

Experiment with different points of view in your narrative. If you're writing in the first person, try switching to the third person, or vice versa. Changing the perspective can completely change the way your words flow. Some stories work better told in first or third person, even second if you're feeling experimental. And when a story works better, it's often easier and faster to write.

A warning: editing existing draft words into a different point of view can be tedious even if it is the best decision for the story (I'm speaking from so, so much experience making this switch mid-draft).

Take a Break

While it would be nice to live every day in a high-octane state of exuberant creativity and maximum word output, creativity needs to be rested.

This might be a total physical rest like sleeping, or just resting your mind with a different, nonmental activity.

Try going for a walk, a gym session, cleaning, cooking, taking a shower, anything physical and mindless. Don't take your phone or headphones with you and let your brain release into a free flow of thought.

Practice Kaleidoscopic Creativity

Kaleidoscopic Creativity, sometimes called "combinatory play" is the idea that engaging with a different artistic activity can enhance the creative capacity for the initial creative intent. For example, stop writing for a while and try painting, or playing music.

This mixing up of disciplines still engages our creative centers but lets the functions of the writing brain relax while still keeping our creativity stimulated. The story goes that Albert Einstein used to play the violin for this purpose.

Read Widely

Expand your reading into something completely different to what you usually read, and something different from what you're currently writing about.

Explore new genres and styles, exposing your thirsty creative mind to new ideas, techniques, and perspectives.

Collaborate

Try bouncing ideas off a friend, writer or otherwise, and asking for their ideas in return. The meshing of two minds can create wild and wonderful ideas neither party might have ever thought of on their own. This phenomenon has been called the Third Mind.

It's quite fun to do this with an AI tool like ChatGPT, if that feels good to you.

Research

Immerse yourself in research related to your novel's themes, settings, or social and or historical context. The knowledge you gain can spark creative ideas and add depth and authority to your work.

Embrace Your Inner Child

Get playful.

What did you enjoy as a kid? Play some old games, listen to old music. Pick up some old hobbies, read picture books or other types of juvenile fiction.

Chances are, what used to drive your play and imagination as a child is still the same thing that drives your creative brain as an adult. It all comes from the same place, after all.

Daydream

Intentionally sit back, or even better, go for a walk, and let your mind wander. Notice what you notice. Think what you think. Try to resist the pressure to "have ideas" while you're doing this. It will happen, but more often than not, the creative breakthrough moments that develop from daydreaming practices happen in the subconscious and pop into consciousness when you're not expecting it.

Journal

There are no limits to what a journaling practice can teach a writer, and boosting creativity is just one of journaling's many benefits.

A journal can be a space to empty the mind of jumbled-up, unhelpful or even untrue thoughts, and see what you really think. Journaling is a great way to uncover what's bothering you, freeing up your brain from the never-ending cycles of worry so it can get on with more important things like creative challenges.

Journaling can also be a space for celebrating what's good in life, what you're grateful for. This does wonders for our positivity, and typically, when we feel good, so does our creativity.

Journaling is also an excellent tool to figure out what's happening in your story. If something isn't working or you're not sure what to write next, take up your journal and write about it. Go over what you do and don't like in the story. Generate lists of possibilities for plots and characters. Journal about what you hope this story will become.

Use Tarot Cards

Tarot is an amazing source of creative inspiration, particularly for writers.

Each tarot card tells a story, and as a whole, a tarot deck creates a narrative, from our foolish naïve beginnings through to an all-knowing state, and all the minutiae of life in between.

Tarot art, even without the card meanings, can be a potent source of inspiration.

For more on using tarot in your writing, check out my work with *Tarot Writers* at www.tarotwriters.com.

Embrace Your Unique Weirdness

Being a writer is an exercise in finding your authenticity, and that starts with embracing your weird, what makes you special, and taking that into your work and everyday living.

Do something weird.

Here are some ideas...

Leave riddles on Post-it notes around your house for your family to solve. Or stick them up in public places.

Insert handwritten letters in library books for the next reader to find.

Lie on the ground in a public place and examine whatever is above you. Parks are a good place to do this. Doing it in shopping malls, for example, might attract the wrong kind of attention, but if that's your thing, go for it.

Make up a new word and slip it casually into a conversation with a friend, no explanation.

Take up an ordinary item and use it for an extraordinary purpose.

If the word "weird" makes you uncomfortable, substitute "unique" or "curios" or "random."

Genre Immersion

Genre immersion is the practice of saturating yourself in anything and everything you can find in the genre you're writing in. Books, TV shows, movies, games, music, art, anything that someone has created that somehow thematically relates to your work in progress.

You're looking at ideas, executions, structures. You're investigating what worked, what didn't, and why. You're hunting for little sparks that make you sit up and go, "Oooh! That's cool!" And then, when you sit down to write your own story, you're looking for new ways to spark those same reactions both in yourself and in your readers.

Yes, you're stealing ideas.

No, this isn't a bad thing.

Borrowing ideas from different sources is where creativity and originality come from. Ideas are like clay. They're really nothing until you work on them, shape them, and bake them, and everyone will produce something totally different from the same raw material.

CHAPTER 11
NARRATIVE STRUCTURE BY THE NUMBERS

50K words is slightly under the average length of a commercial novel, which tend toward the 60-70K range. That said, it is a perfectly acceptable novel length for commercial works, and a novel style narrative fits well into this shorter side of the form.

Nothing is forcing you to follow any structures of formal narrative theory in writing your book. Let your creativity roam about the pages and let the plot fall where it may. That said, if you *do* choose to follow a more traditional style of narrative, it can make things easier to keep your plot and characters on track during this high velocity, wild and wordy ride.

There are so many different approaches and structure maps of narrative theory, this concise book could never list them all. Instead, I'm offering here a breakdown of the basic narrative theory that I've been working with for years, and showing you how to wrangle it into a fifty thousand word container, paced out over a month.

Day	Words
Day 1	1667
Day 2	3334
Day 3	5001
Day 4	6668
Day 5	8335
Day 6	10002
Day 7	11669
Day 8	13336
Day 9	15003
Day 10	16670
Day 11	18337
Day 12	20004
Day 13	21671
Day 14	23338
Day 15	25005
Day 16	26672
Day 17	28339
Day 18	30006
Day 19	31673
Day 20	33340
Day 21	35007
Day 22	36674
Day 23	38341
Day 24	40008
Day 25	41675
Day 26	43342
Day 27	45009
Day 28	46676
Day 29	48343
Day 30	50000 (technically 50010 at 1667 words a day)

THE THREE ACT STRUCTURE

In Western literature, stories mostly operate on a core three act structure.
    1. Beginning.
    2. Middle.
    3. End.

I like to break this down further into a four acts format, where the middle is divided with a story-turning event, usually a moment of decisive change for the main character. It's still three main acts.

1. Beginning
2. Middle Set Up

– BIG EVENT –
3. Middle Consequences
3. Conclusion

1. Beginning
12% - 6000 Words
2. Middle
25% - 12500 Words
50% - 25000
3. End
75% - 37500 words
100% - 50000

ACT 1. BEGINNING

The beginning of the story is the first 25% of the book (days 1 – 8). Roughly.

For your opening 12,500 words your character encounters problems that will begin their character arcs. They are reactive to events and haven't yet fully gained proactive control.

This initial set-up typically breaks down with a hook, inciting incident, and a call to action.

The Hook

The hook is the element of deliciousness that gets your reader into the book. The hook is the little teasing promise to the reader that you're going to give them a story that they will enjoy.

The Inciting Incident

The inciting incident is the is single point in your opening that actually kicks things off. Your inciting incident and your hook can be the same thing, but doesn't have to be. This incident forever alters the character's world. Ensure your inciting incident occurs before 12% of your total word count – 6000 words (day 4).

ACT 2. THE MIDDLE

After encountering the inciting incident, your characters will make a choice and embrace their "call to action." They're officially responding to whatever incited their response in Act 1.

This is the start of the story middle and it happens around 25% (12,500 words, day 8)

The middle is where plots get increasingly complicated. Essentially, it is a process of try, fail, try something new.

For the first half of the middle, your characters react to external situations as they struggle to get what they want.

The middle takes up 50% of the story as a whole.

The Midpoint Shift

At the 50% mark of the story (25K, day 15), your characters encounter something major. This is a plot changing event that, in some way, alters who they are. It's not the climax of the story, but it's the peak of their character arc.

From this shift, your characters know new things or have new skills. They understand what they want and how to get it (but they'll still face conflicts). They shift from reactive to proactive. They have changed forever, but they're still not the person you're setting them up to be at the very end.

As the story now moves towards the 75% mark (37500, day 23), the start of the third act, the stakes increase.

ACT 3. THE END

At 75% (37,500, day 23), you'll be writing your climax. This is the big scene or scenes where everything hangs in the balance and your characters will either succeed or fail.

Over the final 25%, we move through the end, the third act. The climax has happened. Now, how does the world move on from here? At this end, the story stops asking questions and ensures everything gets answered and all the problems are solved. The character understands what they need, perhaps has healed their wounds (or at least understood themselves better), and their character arc is settling them into a whole new person.

Remember this is only a high range view of a basic three-act structure. For a more detailed approach to the ideas in this chapter, you might consider reading my book, *How To Write Your First Novel*.

CHAPTER 12
HOW TO EDIT A MESSY DRAFT

The sun has set on day 30.

You've got 50,000 words of varying quality.

You've also probably got tired hands and a brain a little the worse for wear. You might also have a house in serious need of cleaning, and children whose names you don't quite recall.

So, take a rest and celebrate your victory and let real life gradually creep back in.

Post challenge, some writers continue working on their novels if the story isn't finished. Some maintain the high velocity pace, others slow to tinker at a more sustainable speed.

Some writers close the manuscript at the end of day 30, never think of it again, and happily go back to life as a normal person.

Others look at the wordy pile of mayhem and wonder what to do with it.

This chapter is for the writer who would like to turn that messy Alpha Draft into a real-life novel.

But where do we even begin untangling an actual novel from those words?

Just like writing is done word by word, editing and revising are also best done in small, manageable incremental sections.

So, release that breath. You don't have to fix your pile of words all in one go.

The editing approach outlined in this chapter is a condensed version of the editing section of my book *How To Write Your First Novel*.

THE ELEVEN STEPS TO TURNING A MESSY DRAFT INTO AN ACTUAL NOVEL

1. REMEMBER, IT'S NOT YET A NOVEL

Warning: skipping this step might cause disillusionment, overwhelming disappointment, and misery.

Before you go back and look at the wordy mess you made, remember the first component of the fast drafting mindset.

The title of this book is a misnomer.

At the end of the 30 days, you have not written a novel.

At the end, you have started writing a novel, the most important part of the process, the hardest part of the process. You've got the solid foundation.

Let your messy pile of words be a messy pile of words. Stop projecting the sense that it is meant to be a "novel" yet onto it and you'll be able to approach the revision process with a lot less stress.

2. FINISH IT

Have you written to the end of your story? If not, it's time to finish that first draft. If you have finished, skip to Step 3.

I'm not looking to put you under more stress, but it can often be the best thing to continue writing your novel until the end with the same fast-paced fervor that you used during the 30 day challenge. It's not vital, but it's more likely to ensure a consistency of style and tone throughout the draft. Also, you'll get it done faster. If 1,667 a day is too much for everyday life, lessen as necessary.

The story must be complete. It doesn't need to be fully cohesive, but it needs to have a sense of beginning, middle, and end.

The Alpha Draft should also be about the length you'll want your finished novel to be, but that's flexible as you will add and cut words throughout the revision process.

3. DO SOMETHING ELSE

Once you're at the end of the story and have something vaguely resembling a start, middle, and end, leave it alone.

Do something totally unrelated to your novel. Write a different story. Hang out with your family and friends. Focus on your day job. Play games. Work out. Whatever. Live a normal life without touching that manuscript. Let your story rest. During this process, your story will simmer and ripen in your subconscious and when you're ready to come back to it, you'll be able to look at it with a range of completely fresh perspectives and ideas. Some authors do this for a few days, others for weeks. It's up to you.

4. READ IT

When you're sufficiently rested, take your manuscript and read it.

Print it out if you like. Send it to your e-reader.

Read it like you would read any other novel, beginning to end.

Don't edit anything.

Here, you're familiarizing yourself with the ideas, the world you created, and the good intentions you had for the story that the messy word pile might not have fully captured yet.

NOTE:

Think of the following editing steps as like a pyramid. On the bottom, the steps target the big foundational stuff like plot structure and characterization. As we reach higher up the pyramid, we get into less foundational things like physical description, higher still until we're into finer micro details like polishing word choices, and proof-reading for grammar and typos.

5. BIG PICTURE EDITS – REVISING FOR STRUCTURE

This is where you make sure you've got a character arc and have that narrative structure in place.

We're still not worrying about typos yet, but I do often correct anything that's sorely wrong.

Go back to the beginning and start reading. Yes, this time you make your changes.

What is your hook? What and where is your inciting incident?

Make sure your major plot points occur at the right time during the story.

Does your story make sense overall?

Does the character arc make sense? Is your character changing? Have you given them flaws and some motivating factor that haunts them? Do they realize something about themselves?

You can do one pass for plot structure and one for character arc, but as these two elements of narrative are so closely entwined, it can be a good idea to tackle them at the same time.

In this pass, I'll also make sure all characters generally act and react in the context of their personality, but we'll do a dedicated character action pass soon.

6. REVISE FOR SETTING AND WORLD-BUILDING

In this step, we're looking at your story location.

Where is everything happening? How are the characters interacting with their environments?

Is everything happening where it should be happening? Is everyone in the right place?

Have you described your setting appropriately?

If your story takes place in a real-life location, do any additional research and add in any details you need to really bring your story to life. Remember, even fantastical places require real-world reality, so now check how credible your world-building is.

During this pass, pay special attention to how time moves within your story. Do you have characters doing an impossible number of things in one day? Is travel time realistic? Have characters had time to sleep at some point? Had time to eat, even if it's not shown? How do you mark the passing of time in your story world?

7. REVISE FOR SCENE STRUCTURE

The structure of an individual scene echoes that of an entire novel. It starts with an inciting incident, and it moves through to a midpoint shift. Complications happen, and then everything culminates in action or revelation.

Something needs to happen in every scene. Every scene needs to drive the whole story along through the flow of consequences. Now's the time to make sure that happens. Any scene that doesn't change and move the story forward gets revised or cut out.

If you're writing to express a particular theme or have a moral or message in your story, this is where you make sure it flows through every scene.

Check your foreshadowing here too. Do you want to give your readers a hint of what's coming? Put in little details like conveniently placed weapons that might save the day by chance in the final fight scene, or seemingly insignificant details your character suddenly remembers from the story beginning that will crack the case wide open in the end. Weave it all into the earlier scenes now.

8. REVISE FOR CHARACTER ACTIONS

This refers to the little physical actions that pepper scenes. What are people doing as they're talking, thinking, etc.? I've heard this referred to as the Visceral Pass as it shows in a more physical sense what characters are going through.

In many a writer's Alpha Drafts, characters will do a lot of nodding and smiling, sometimes grimacing, and not much else every single time they speak. There's also a lot of staring and shrugging.

In this pass, make sure they're moving and acting like human beings. Give them little tasks to do, let them physically interact with others and their environment, make sure their physical reactions reflect what's happening in the scene.

This is also the time to make sure that your characters are speaking distinctly. In real life, everyone speaks differently, so make sure this comes across in your work. An excellent way to do this is to make sure you can tell who is talking just from the dialogue without any "she/he/they said" attribution tags.

9. POLISH THE PROSE

By now, your manuscript essentially has everything it needs. Next, we turn to making the smaller components work. Here we look at paragraphs, making sure the right scene emphasis happens at the right paragraph points and also sentence structure.

Balance long, flowing sentences with short, punchy sentences.

Also, pay attention here to the white space on the page. If you've got massive chunks of text stretching across the page for more than one or two paragraphs, then revise to include some dialogue or break it up into shorter paragraphs.

Reading your work out loud also helps at this point.

As you edit these small details, also keep an eye out for anything you might have missed in the last passes.

Have you repeated the same points in different words? Are there unnecessary details, or trivialities that do nothing to serve your plots and characters?

This is the phase to tighten up all your scenes, paragraphs, and sentences to ensure every word is working in your favor. General guidelines suggest cutting ten percent of the total number of words, but this is highly variable.

Try not to repeat words too close to one another or have too many similar-sounding words in one sentence unless it's for a particular effect.

Make sure your character names are all very different. A Tom and a Tony or an Adele and an Amelie together will often confuse readers.

As you read, pretend you're performing for an audiobook or live reading at your novel launch. It not only helps to fine-tune your prose, it's also fun!

10. TYPOS AND LINE EDITING

You might have taken care of most of this in the last pass, but do one more read-through to make sure it's all good. Take care of all the colored squiggles in your document by doing the spelling and grammar checks. Be on the lookout for those words like homonyms or autocorrect replacements that basic spell check doesn't find.

This is the time for a program like ProWritingAid or Grammarly to work their magic.

11. FINAL CHECKS

At this stage, you'll have a finished novel. But there's always something. Keep reading until you think there's nothing left to change.

This is the point I bring my manuscripts to before I show them to anyone else, be that beta readers, critique partners, or editors. These phases are beyond the scope of this book, but when you're ready, you'll find a world of information on editors and publishing waiting for you.

AFTERWORD

I have 50K novel in a month writing challenges to thank for my entire career.

The Fast Drafting philosophy I've shared in this book made me a writer and taught me that writing a novel doesn't have to be some colossal undertaking that takes years of painstaking effort, available only for the select few in their ivory tower of literary grandeur.

Fast Drafting a novel in a month taught me how to have fun with writing, how to push myself beyond what I thought was possible. I would never have written any novel without it, let alone multiple.

It's my every hope that this adventure does the same for you.

Have fun.

Write a lot.

Repeat.

Write well.

X Kate

ABOUT THE AUTHOR

Kate Krake writes magical and otherworldly fiction, as well as nonfiction designed to support and inspire her fellow writers.

She is passionate about folklore, pop culture, long distance walking, tarot, and curious trivia. She can usually be found with her nose in a book, her ears in a song, and her head in the clouds.

Kate has lived all over Australia and currently lives in Perth, Australia, with her family.

Connect

www.katekrake.com
kate@katekrake.com

BOOKS BY KATE KRAKE

NONFICTION

THE CREATIVE WRITING LIFE

A Writer's Creativity

A Writer's Practice

A Writer's Mindset

The Creative Rebellion

Journaling For Writers

How To Be A Better Writer

Write Your Novel In A Month

How To Write Your First Novel

Writing Beyond Fear

The Writer's Book of Joy

The Writer's Book of Weird

TAROT WRITERS

Tarot For Writers

Tarot Spreads For Writers

Tarot Meanings For Writers

Author Arcana: A Tarot Journal For Writers

FICTION

Witch Against Wicked
Witchy Small-Town Fantasy Series

A Maze of Magic

A Mask of Chaos

A Trial of Ghosts

A Wreath of Ruin

A Hex of Wolves

A Trick of Bones

A Coven of Ravens

Shifter Mates of Fairbright Falls
Small-Town Shifter Paranormal Romance Series

Kissing Kitty

Good Luck Griffin

Coyote Serenade

The Unicorn's Love Story

Magic Works
Standalone Contemporary Fantasy Novels

The Elm Witch

Night Shift At The Shadow Bay Hotel

Magical and Otherworldly Short Stories

Familiar Shadows of the Strange: Surreal Stories of Uncanny Magic
Surrealist and magical realism short stories

Creatures of the Liminal Wilds
Fantasy and sci-fi cryptid short stories

Copyright 2025 Kate Krake
All rights reserved.

Some content in this book was originally published as *The Nanowrimo Survival Guide* (2023).

Inkwell & Elm is an imprint of
Krakenfire Media

The author publisher shall not be held liable or responsible for any loss or damage allegedly arising from any suggestion or information contained in this book. No guarantee or other promise is made as to any results that may be obtained from using the content of this book.
This information in this book does not replace professional medical, psychological, legal, financial, business opinion and advice on any occasion.

Cover Design by 1111 Studio

Any administrative inquiries regarding this book should be directed to Krakenfire Media admin@krakenfiremedia.com